Racism and Ethnic Bias

Racism and Ethnic Bias

Everybody's Problem

Linda Jacobs Altman

Enslow Publishers, Inc.

40 Industrial Road	PO Box 38
Box 398	Aldershot
Berkeley Heights, NJ 07922	Hants GU12 6BP
USA	UK

http://www.enslow.com

Library of Congress Cataloging-in-Publication Data

Altman, Linda Jacobs, 1943-
    Racism and ethnic bias : everybody's problem / Linda Jacobs Altman.
        p. cm. — (Teen issues)
    Includes bibliographical references and index.
    ISBN 0-7660-1578-5 (hardcover)
    1. Racism—Juvenile literature. 2. Racism—United States—Juvenile literature.
3. Stereotype (Psychology)—Juvenile literature. 4. Race relations—Juvenile
literature. 5. United States—Race relations—Juvenile literature. [1. Racism.
2. Stereotype (Psychology) 3. Race relations. 4. Racially mixed people.] I. Title. II.
Series.
    HT1521 .A45   2001
    305.8'00973—dc21   00-012460

Printed in the United States of America

10 9 8 7 6 5 4 3 2 1

To Our Readers:
We have done our best to make sure all Internet addresses in this book were active and appropriate when we went to press. However, the author and the publisher have no control over and assume no liability for the material available on those Internet sites or on other Web sites they may link to. Any comments or suggestions can be sent by e-mail to comments@enslow.com or to the address on the back cover.

Illustration Credits: *Lake County Record Bee*, p. 52; Library of Congress, pp. 13, 16, 22, 24, 32, 37, 42; © 2000 Stan Badz/PGA Tour, p. 48.

Cover Photo: © Skjold Photos; background © Corel Corporation.

Contents

1

What Is Racism?

In 1998, David Calvin James of Phoenix, Arizona, was walking down the street minding his own business when two police officers stopped him. James, an African-American tool-and-die maker with no criminal record, found himself thrust into a nightmare. The officers sprayed pepper spray into his face and beat him so badly that his left arm was permanently damaged. Then they hauled him off to jail. He was later released for lack of evidence, but the damage had already been done.

In January 2000, James sued the Phoenix Police Department for damages, stating that he had been the victim of a controversial practice known as racial profiling. A profile is a list of characteristics thought to be typical of certain types of criminals. Law enforcement officers use it to identify "suspicious" people who ought to be stopped and questioned.

Many innocent people of color find themselves targets of this practice. They are watched more carefully in department stores because they are thought to be shoplifters. They are stopped on the highway because they might be car thieves or drug runners. David Calvin James did not come under suspicion because of anything he had done. "He was in a drug area, walking alone and he was black," said his attorney.[1] In Phoenix that night, race was reason enough to violate a man's civil rights.

Racial Classification

The idea of race began as a means of classifying and categorizing human beings. In 1738, Swedish biologist Carolus Linnaeus divided humankind into four basic racial groups. His divisions were based upon geography and skin color: the familiar red, yellow, black, and white. Thus, there were red people in the Americas, yellow people in Asia, black people in Africa, and white people in Europe.

In the nineteenth and early twentieth centuries, scientists studied the characteristics of each race. They considered such factors as hair texture, facial appearance, and physical proportions. They soon discovered that there was as much variation within racial groups as among them.

For example, the bushmen of Africa's Kalahari Desert are small and golden-brown in skin color; the Masai are tall and dark-skinned. Both are classed as black Africans. Caucasians, or whites, exhibit similar differences. There are blond, blue-eyed people in Northern Europe, and shorter, dark-haired people in the south.

Attempts to classify everyone resulted in a great deal of confusion. There were categories, subcategories, and "mini-races." Also, ethnic groups were often confused with races. For example, in the early twentieth century, Italians, Irish, and Jews were considered races.

Race and Ethnicity

In the confusion between race and ethnicity, learned behaviors were sometimes classified as inborn biological traits. This often happened when Europeans observed the habits of people they considered "primitive." For example, the fact that many Africans and American Indians lived in tribal cultures "proved" that they were incapable of creating more complex societies. This in turn indicated that dark-skinned races were less intelligent and capable than whites.

The members of an ethnic group usually share language or dialect, religion, and cultural traditions. They express group solidarity through such things as the foods they eat, the clothes they wear, the songs they sing, and the games they play.

Race may or may not be part of ethnicity. The American Anthropological Association (AAA) scientists, who study the ways of human groups, explained how race and ethnicity interact:

> Populations with similar physical appearances may have different ethnic identities (Serb and Croat, or Hutu and Tutsi), and populations with different physical appearances may have a common ethnic identity (for example, many Caribbean Islanders have roots in different parts of Asia, Africa and Europe, yet everyone on a particular island is considered, for example, a Jamaican, Trinidadian, etc.).[2]

The Biology of Race

In the late twentieth century, geneticists (scientists who study the mechanisms of heredity) shed new light on old questions about race. Their findings showed that race was quite literally "skin deep." The obvious differences in skin color and other physical traits can be better explained by geography than genetics. Anthropologist Bernard G. Campbell explained:

> Such physical characteristics as tallness and shortness, dark skin and light skin, straight hair and curly hair, [evolved] during the millennia when the human body had to accommodate itself to heat and cold and to the variations of sunlight in different latitudes. The relatively short, thick body of the Eskimo, for instance, conserves heat better than the tall, thin bodies of some [Africans], which present a much greater area of skin to be cooled by the air. Similarly, thick, straight hair . . . might help to maintain the temperature of the brain in cold climates, whereas tightly curled hair seems an adaptation guarding against hot tropical sunshine; it is a noticeable characteristic of genetically unrelated peoples in Africa and the islands of Southeast Asia and the South Pacific.[3]

In the late 1990s, research into the human genetic code revealed important new information about race and human differences. Of the thirty thousand to forty thousand genes that make up a human being, 99.9 percent are the same in people of all races. They create the characteristics all humans share.

The remaining 0.1 percent produce individual differences. They are the reason that no two people, with the exception of identical twins, are exactly alike. Only a few of those genes produce racial traits. According to the

American Anthropological Association, this means that "there is a greater variation within 'racial' groups than between them."[4]

Differences such as skin color and eye shape do not justify "race" as basic biological category. Anthropologists therefore concluded that race is not a true physical category at all. It is a social and cultural division. In other words, race is much like ethnicity: A set of categories created by human beings to distinguish one group from another.

In the late twentieth century, many anthropologists concluded that race is not a true physical category at all. It is a social and cultural division. In other words, race is much like ethnicity: a set of categories created by human beings to distinguish one group from another.

This does not mean that race is unreal. It does mean that race is not as important as people have believed it to be. Anthropologists now accept that as scientific fact. Unfortunately, many people do not. Those who hold bigoted opinions continue to believe that race is very important indeed.

Bigotry is commonly defined as belief in the superiority of one's own group, combined with intolerance for those who differ. A bigot's world is small, with no room for strangers. It does have room for prejudices of all kinds, and for that peculiar form of hatred known as racism.

The Foundations of Racism

Racism begins with the belief that race shapes personality, character, intelligence, and ability. It therefore defines human groups and indicates their worth. That idea has been used to justify any number of evils, from conquest and colonialism to slavery and mass slaughter.

The colonizing empires of the fifteenth and sixteenth centuries used racism to justify conquering American Indians and other "primitive" people. The founding fathers of America used it to build racial and ethnic discrimination into the very fabric of their new society.

Those ringing words that start the Declaration of Independence—"that all men are created equal; that they are endowed by their creator with certain inalienable rights; that among these are life, liberty, & the pursuit of happiness"—did not apply to American Indians or enslaved Africans. These groups were considered inferior to whites. Therefore, they were not entitled to the same "inalienable rights."

Even those who opposed slavery on moral grounds often continued to believe in white superiority. For example, Thomas Jefferson called slavery a "cruel war against human nature itself, violating its most sacred rights of life and liberty."[5] He wanted to end slavery, but not to accept black people as the equals of whites.

He considered blacks inferior to whites in most respects. He expressed this clearly in *Notes on the State of Virginia.* In it, Jefferson wrote that black people are less intelligent and imaginative than whites.[6]

Jefferson's observations demonstrate the workings of racial prejudice. Prejudice is an idea formed about an entire class of people and then applied to all of the members of that class. Individual differences are either ignored or explained away.

For example, Jefferson belittled the writings of former slave Ignatius Sancho. He also suggested that they might have been done by someone else: "Upon the whole, though we admit [Sancho] to the first place among those of his own colour . . . when we compare him with [white writers] . . . we are compelled to enroll him at the bottom of the column. This criticism supposes the letters published under his name to be genuine, and to have received amendment from no other hand."[7]

Ideas that are prejudiced often lead to discriminatory acts. Discrimination is usually defined as treatment based on class or category rather than individual merit. For example, believing that black people are inferior is a prejudiced idea; forcing black children to attend racially segregated schools is a discriminatory act. Prejudice and discrimination separate people into mutually hostile groups, producing hatred, fear, and injustice.

In their hoods and flowing robes, members of the Ku Klux Klan terrorized black people and other minorities at the end of the Civil War and again in the twentieth century.

Racism and Intelligence

One of the most common prejudices about people of color is that they are less intelligent than whites. Racists believe that this explains their "primitive" cultures and supposed inability to reason.

Scottish philosopher David Hume (1711–1776), an older contemporary of Thomas Jefferson, reflected this view in his writings:

> I am apt to suspect the negroes and in general all the other species of men (for there are four or five different kinds) to be naturally inferior to the whites. There never was a civilized nation of any other complexion than white, or even any individual eminent either in action or [thought]. No ingenious [inventions] among them, no arts, no sciences. On the other hand, the most rude and barbarous of the whites . . . have still something eminent about them, in their [courage], form of government, or some other particular."[8]

Those ideas have been echoed for generations. By the 1990s, some people believed—or at least hoped—that these ideas were passing out of favor. Then in 1994, psychologist Richard J. Herrnstein and research fellow Charles Murray published *The Bell Curve: Intelligence and Class Structure in American Life.*[9] The book restated the old arguments about intelligence, especially in regard to black people. Among other things, the authors claimed that whites averaged a score of 100 on standard intelligence tests, while blacks averaged only 85. They further claimed that this difference in intelligence was inborn and therefore unchangeable.

Herrnstein and Murray came under fire both for their conclusions and their methods. Their work was based on comparisons of Intelligence Quotient (IQ) test scores. IQ tests are supposed to measure the ability to think and learn, not how much a person already knows. Actually, test results are strongly influenced by the subject's level of education, familiarity with the culture, and command of language.

The bell curve study put a modern face on an old argument. Like the whites who enslaved Africans and conquered American Indians, Herrnstein and Murray claimed that the white race was superior to all others. Whites were therefore entitled to dominate people of color.

Institutionalized Racism

In the United States, white dominance is a normal part of everyday life. White people, mostly males, control government, business, industry, education, and professions such as medicine and law. They control the media, from neighborhood newspapers to television networks, movie studios, and the brave new world of cyberspace.

This is institutional racism, or racism that is built into the foundations of society. It results in white privilege, a condition in which white people benefit simply because of the color of their skin. It excludes or makes people of color seem to matter less than Caucasians.

According to Victor Rodriguez, a professor at Concordia University in California, only 5 percent of the top executives of major corporations are women or people of color. This lack of power makes a huge difference, as Rodriguez points out:

> Let's say I work as a janitor and I'm racially prejudiced. Maybe I can do something negative like not pick up your garbage. Will it seriously damage your standard of living? Obviously not. But what if I'm a personnel director and . . . I [see] you as being less qualified than a white person? That's probably going to affect the remainder of your life. That's the difference."[10]

Institutionalized racism does not have to be based upon

Adolf Hitler's vision of a "racial state" was responsible for the mass murder of six million Jews and at least five million others who were considered "subhuman."

hatred. It simply assumes white superiority in all things. Under certain conditions, this assumption can become the foundation for all manner of horrors, from slavery or random hate crimes to all-out genocide.

Racism and Genocide

Long before *The Bell Curve*, similar ideas about white superiority became the foundation for genocide, the systematic killing of entire peoples. During the years that Adolf Hitler ruled Germany (1933 to 1945), his Nazi party killed 6 million Jews and about 5 million others who were classed as "subhumans."

This genocide was part of Hitler's plan to build a German "master race" through eugenics, or selective breeding. To do this, he made "racial purity" the watchword of an entire society. Germans who married or mated across racial lines could be imprisoned or even executed. Those with mental retardation, mental illness, or other disabilities were killed in euthanasia, or "mercy death," centers. Those who were believed to have hereditary defects were forcibly sterilized so they could not produce children. Those who met the Nazi ideal were encouraged—and even required—to have as many children as possible.

The horrors of the Nazi "racial state" are an extreme example of what can happen when racism becomes social policy. Hitler's reich, or empire, was destroyed in a long and costly war. Unfortunately, the racism behind that empire was not destroyed.

In the twenty-first century, self-styled white supremacists cling to the notion that the white race is superior to all others. This bigotry extends beyond race to include people who are different because of ethnicity, religion, or sexual orientation.

The goal of these white supremacists is to create a society in which people of color and other minorities will have no voice.

The goal of those who work for racial justice is to see that this does not happen. No one really knows how this conflict will be resolved. However, one thing is clear. Its outcome may well determine how the races live together for generations to come.

2

Stereotyping

The word *stereotype* once referred to a mold that was used to make identical copies of a single object. In 1922, journalist Walter Lippmann used the word to describe standardized, "cookie-cutter" images and perceptions of particular groups. Racial and ethnic stereotypes abound in American society: Latinos are "hot-tempered" and lazy; African Americans hang out on ghetto street corners and deal drugs; Asians are secretive, deceitful, and clannish.

The Characteristics of Stereotypes
Walter Lippmann's stereotypes attracted the notice of cognitive psychologists, who are scientists concerned with human thought processes. Study after study confirmed

Lippmann's description: Stereotypes are simple, secondhand, always false, and resistant to change.

Simplicity is the most basic feature of stereotypes. They reduce complex realities to brief descriptions, the way a cartoon sketch reduces physical features to a few lines.

These simplified images are part of the reason why some people think members of other groups "all look alike." For example, a white person seeing Asians might notice only those characteristics that are part of the stereotype: short stature, dark, straight hair, almond-shaped eyes, skin with a faintly yellow or tawny cast. Judged by those characteristics alone, Asians *do* look a great deal alike. The same holds true for members of any other group with identifiable physical traits.

The second characteristic of stereotypes is that they are not based upon firsthand experience. They are built from images in the surrounding culture. These images are everywhere: at home, in the classroom and the workplace, on the street, and on television. Everyone is exposed to them at a very young age.

A white child who has never met an American Indian will still "know" a great deal about American Indians as a group. The old stereotype is that they wear feather headdresses, paint their faces for war, attack wagon trains, and live in tents called tepees.

The modern version of this stereotype is that American Indians become people who live on reservations, drive beat-up trucks, stay drunk a good deal of the time, and cannot hold down a job. Either way, the stereotype gives a false picture of American Indians.

The third characteristic of stereotypes is that they are always false. They thrive on all-or-nothing thinking: "All white people are racists," "All black people live in inner-city ghettos and deal drugs," "All Japanese people are treacherous and deceitful."

A statement about all members of a group cannot possibly be true; even one exception is enough to disprove it. Given the broad individual differences within groups, there are always exceptions.

Bigots often try to "explain" these exceptions in a way that will keep the stereotype intact. For example, professor of anatomy Wesley Critz George once explained the existence of intelligent black people by remarking that "One swallow does not make a summer, and a few intelligent Negroes do not make a race."[1]

This type of thinking is what gives stereotypes their staying power; what Walter Lippmann described as their resistance to change. Stereotypes survive despite logic and evidence to the contrary. Once fixed in people's minds, the stereotypes operate without logic or conscious thought.

Though stereotypes can rarely be changed by logic, they do adapt to changing conditions within society. When a particular stereotype becomes outdated, new features are added. The evolution of American Indian stereotypes is a good example of this. In the popular imagination, American Indians went from attacking wagon trains to driving rattletrap trucks and getting drunk. The images changed to keep up with the times; the prejudice behind those images remained intact.

African-American stereotypes went through similar changes. During slavery and for some time afterward, black people were regarded as simple-minded primitives who lacked both intelligence and common sense. By the late twentieth century, they had become jive-talking ghetto toughs, listening to rap music on enormous boom boxes and mugging innocent people in the streets. Both images reflect white belief in black inferiority.

In the nineteenth century, American Indians were stereotyped as violence-prone "savages" who drank too much.

Social upheavals such as economic collapse or war can give new life to old stereotypes. For example, when the United States went to war with Japan in 1941, Japanese stereotypes led to one of the worst human rights violations in United States history. By order of President Franklin D. Roosevelt, Americans of Japanese ancestry were rounded up and put into prison camps.

Many of these people were native-born Americans who had never even seen Japan. Many were too old or too young to represent a danger to the nation. That made no difference. They were all "enemy aliens" who could not be trusted.

The internment lasted until the end of the war. Many Japanese Americans lost their homes and businesses while they were in the camps. They had to start over, rebuilding their lives piece by piece.

Stereotyping and Categorizing

Psychologists once believed that only bigoted people used stereotypes. In the 1970s, they discovered that this was not true. Stereotypes grow out of the human need for order and structure. Everybody uses them.

The ability to organize information into meaningful categories is an important part of human intelligence. It helps people to make sense of their world. Stereotypes serve the same function, but they do it poorly; psychologist John Bargh once described them as "categories that have gone too far."[2]

One of the reasons stereotypes endure despite their weaknesses is that they often contain a grain of truth or at least the appearance of truth. A stereotype worthy of the name is likely to be true of at least some people at some times. For example, some African Americans really do live

The stereotype of the African-American slave was of someone ignorant and generally content with his or her lot in life.

in ghettos and deal drugs, and some white Americans are hate-filled racists.

To people who are prejudiced, the grain of truth in these stereotypes becomes "evidence" of their accuracy. Those who believe that whites are racists cite groups like the Ku Klux Klan or Aryan Nations. Those who believe that blacks are ghetto-dwelling drug dealers point to police raids on ghetto "crack houses."

In some cases, the grain of truth lies in a mistake. This often happens when people judge other cultures by the standards of their own. For example, some people believe that Mexicans are "shifty" because they do not look a person in the eye. White Americans tend to value eye contact as evidence of sincerity and truthfulness. In Mexican culture, lowering the eyes is a sign of respect. It is rude to stare into the face of a stranger, an elder, or someone in a position of authority.

Unfortunately, knowing this may not prevent negative reactions. Some actions can seem "wrong" no matter how much one knows about them. They trigger negative stereotypes that become a barrier to communication. Often, the person will not be aware that this is happening. He or she simply feels uncomfortable without knowing why.

Stereotypes that are based on cultural mistakes can function differently in different environments. An anonymous commentator once called this the "when in Rome do as the Romans do" effect. For example, a white American in the United States might be annoyed when a Mexican acquaintance lowers his gaze. In Mexico, that American might consider the same behavior perfectly appropriate.

People who spend time in foreign cultures are familiar with this effect. When a particular behavior begins to seem "normal" it no longer triggers the stereotypical response.

However, the stereotype will often return and be as strong as ever when the individual is back on home ground.

Stereotypes in Popular Culture and the Media

In twenty-first-century America, movies, television, and other mass media have become the core of popular culture. They create fads and fashions, focus public attention on social issues, shape cultural values, and make superstars of athletes, actors, commentators, and other public figures. They preserve old stereotypes and create new ones. They can also establish countertypes, or "reverse stereotypes," that can change the way people think about race.

With this power to shape public opinion comes a responsibility that many media representatives may not want. They become accountable for the images they create. This can sometimes lead to controversy and embarrassment.

For example, filmmaker George Lucas was criticized for the comic-relief character Jar-Jar Binks in the movie *Star Wars: The Phantom Menace*. Many people protested that the character was insulting to African Americans. They pointed out that Jar-Jar's speech was a parody of black Caribbean dialect. He was loose-limbed, hopelessly clumsy, and none too bright. Lucas supporters countered that Jar-Jar was simply a fantasy character who did not represent any human group.

In the early days of movies and television, nobody would have bothered to protest a character like Jar-Jar Binks. Stereotypes were everywhere in the media, and they were accepted as normal. African Americans were portrayed as railroad porters or household maids. American Indians had parts as bloodthirsty savages. In other movies, Latinos were depicted as outlaw bandits or given roles of chronically sleepy ne'er-do-wells. Asians ran laundries and spoke a choppy kind of English.

Whites were also stereotyped. Offscreen, white actors could become superstars. People of color could not. Onscreen, white characters could be heroes or villains, but their whiteness made them "normal." The media was a bastion of white power and white privilege. It reflected the institutional racism of the larger society.

Not until the late 1960s did this begin to change. Racial and ethnic minorities began to appear in less stereotypical roles. The countertype appeared to challenge the old, negative stereotypes.

The so-called "blacksploitation" films of the 1970s featured strong African-American heroes in action movies filled with car chases, explosions, shoot-outs, and general mayhem. Nobody would have mistaken these films for great art, but they did feature black actors in roles that had formerly been played only by whites.

The first of these films, *Shaft*, starred Richard Roundtree as the perfect countertype to images of African Americans as servile and dull-witted. Hero John Shaft was a smart, street-savvy private detective who could mix it up with the best of them. His appeal crossed racial lines to draw sizable white audiences.

A number of other minority actors, athletes, commentators, and singers proved they could reach people of all races and ethnicities. Most of these crossover personalities were African American. Other racial and ethnic groups were generally less visible, at least in the top ranks of stardom.

Important as they were, these positive images could not destroy older stereotypes or end racism in the media. At the end of the 2000 television season, journalist Jonathan Storm saw what he called "a stunning racial chasm" in viewing patterns. The Nielsen ratings revealed that "seven of the 10

TV shows most watched by African Americans are also the seven programs that come in dead last among whites."[3]

Psychologists have generally given up the idea that stereotyping can be eliminated. Human beings create stereotypes because it is natural for them to do so. It is the way the human mind functions, and that cannot be changed. However, the content of those stereotypes is a product of culture. It is learned, and can therefore be unlearned. According to an article in *Psychology Today,* "some stereotype researchers think that the solution to automatic stereotyping lies in the process itself. Though practice, they say, people can weaken the mental links that connect minorities to negative stereotypes and strengthen the ones that connect them to positive conscious beliefs."[4]

Even without negative images, racial and ethnic stereotypes would be simplified and largely inaccurate. That is their nature. However, they would not tend to portray whole groups of people as unworthy and inferior. This in itself would be a major victory in the struggle for racial and social justice.

3

Bridging the Racial Divide

Being a member of a racial or ethnic minority in a society that is race conscious is not easy. In white America, nonwhites do not have the luxury of defining themselves apart from race. Skin color or some other distinguishing feature becomes part of their identity. A black person who becomes a doctor, for example, will be known as a black doctor. A white doctor is simply a doctor.

This is as true in the twenty-first century as it was in the twentieth and before. It is true in spite of laws that ended racial segregation and established equal opportunity programs for minorities. No law can wipe out the underlying racism that identifies and classifies people by the color of their skin.

Coping with this racism is still a normal part of life for racial and ethnic minorities. Even those who do not have to face open hatred cannot escape institutionalized racism. They grow up on the "wrong" side of a racial divide, expecting to be denied privileges white people take for granted and to be scapegoated, or unfairly blamed, for the ills of society.

The Privileges of Being White

People of color are painfully aware of the privileges that come with whiteness. Most white people are not. They simply do not see all the little things that make life easier on their side of the racial divide. "White privilege is not something I get to decide whether I want to keep," wrote journalism professor Robert Jensen. "Every time I walk into a store at the same time as a black man and the security guard follows him and leaves me alone to shop, I am benefitting from white privilege."[1]

The social and economic benefits of white privilege are enormous. Middle-class whites benefit from the accumulated wealth and social status of their families. People of color are more likely to become trapped in lower socioeconomic circumstances.

In a 1995 study, scholars Melvin Oliver and Thomas Shapiro found a huge economic gap. For every dollar held by whites, African Americans have only fifteen cents.[2] Black poverty, like the institutionalized racism that causes it, is a major feature of American society.

Another feature is not so easy to identify or describe. It has to do with the role race plays in everyday life. White people do not have to think about their own skin color as they go about daily routines. Black people cannot afford to forget.

Journalist David Shipler gives a revealing example of black racial awareness in his book A Country of Strangers:

"When Richard Orange was a boy, he made a deposit in his savings account, then ran out of the bank to catch a bus. 'My father slapped me,' he remembered. He said, 'Never run out of a bank!' Today, at forty-two, I never run out of a bank, I never run out of a store."[3]

For people of color, such precautions are both routine and necessary. Unfortunately, they are not always effective. In times of crisis, when mainstream society needs someone to blame, minorities make convenient scapegoats.

Scapegoats and Whipping Boys

The term *scapegoat* comes from an ancient Hebrew ritual in which a sacrificial goat was burdened with the sins of the people and driven into the wilderness. Today, it has come to mean a person or group that is unfairly blamed for the misdeeds of others or for disasters beyond anyone's control.

People scapegoat for many reasons: to atone for sin, prevent evil, escape punishment, or justify aggression against real or imagined enemies. Scapegoating can also provide seemingly reasonable explanations for the uncertainties and misfortunes of life.

The scapegoat may be a real or imagined enemy or an innocent substitute who is punished for the crimes of others. The choice generally depends upon the need. A nation at war needs enemies to hate. A person burdened with guilt needs someone to bear the blame.

Long ago in Europe, this blame-bearer was chosen as a scapegoat for children of the royal household. Giving a prince a good spanking was unthinkable. One did not strike a child who might someday be king. At the same time, bad deeds could not be allowed to go unpunished. The royal houses solved this problem in an interesting way.

In a sensational trial that rocked the French military in the nineteenth century, Captain Alfred Dreyfus was condemned to life imprisonment, a victim of anti-Semitic scapegoating.

Each prince had a "whipping boy" who took his blows. Thus the prince was punished vicariously, through a substitute.

The scapegoating of people known to be innocent or harmless was often associated with sacrificial rituals. For example, the Aztecs of Mexico kept prisoners of war to use in their human sacrifices. The ancient Athenians fed and clothed a number of homeless people for the same purpose. When the Athenians needed to appease their gods to prevent or stop some disaster, they had a ready pool of potential sacrifices close at hand.

In a classic short story called *The Lottery*, horror writer Shirley Jackson created a chilling portrait of a town on the day of its annual purification ritual. The story opens with the citizens assembling in the village square. Jackson creates a sense of lurking evil beneath descriptions of ordinary events: neighbors chatting pleasantly about one thing and another, children playing with stones that they pile in one corner of the square.

Then one man produces a battered box and calls the townsfolk forward. Quietly, with no apparent fear, heads of households file past and draw out folded slips of paper for each family member. The atmosphere becomes tense as the people open their papers and look around to see who has drawn the one that is marked with a black spot. When the woman is identified, her neighbors and even her own family begin moving away from her. Without apology or seeming regret, they pick up stones from the pile the children have made:

> Tessie Hutchinson . . . held her hands out desperately as the villagers moved in on her. "It isn't fair," she said. A stone hit her on the side of the head.

Old Man Warner was saying, "Come on, come on, everyone." Steve Adams was in the front of the crowd of villagers, with Mrs. Graves beside him.

"It isn't fair, it isn't right," Mrs. Hutchinson screamed, and then they were upon her.[4]

There the story ends. Since it first appeared in a 1948 issue of *The New Yorker*, generations of readers have expressed opinions about what makes the end of the story so horrifying. Some say it is the senseless death of an innocent victim. Others believe it is the ease with which decent, ordinary people turned into remorseless killers.

The Evil Enemy

When the scapegoat is an enemy rather than an innocent substitute, people react with rage and hatred. Demagogues, leaders who prey upon the fears of the masses, have always known this. There is no easier way to rally the people than to give them a clearly defined enemy who poses a clearly defined threat.

As an article in the online political affairs magazine *The Public Eye* explains, scapegoating the enemy involves "pitting the familiar 'in group' against the alien 'out group.'"[5] The enemy is stripped of personal identity and humanness, then demonized into a thing of unspeakable evil.

Hatred of these "monsters" is not only allowed but is also a patriotic duty. Bound by this shared hatred, members of the in group see themselves as heroes in a noble cause. This is the mentality that produces hate crimes, terrorism, and wars of "ethnic cleansing."

Racial and ethnic minorities are not the only victims of this process. People are also targeted for other reasons, including their religious beliefs, political opinions, or sexual orientation. American history alone is filled with examples, from the witch hunts of the seventeenth century to the anti-communist hysteria of the twentieth. In the 1980s, the appearance of AIDS led to widespread gay-bashing, or persecution of homosexuals.

AIDS is a deadly and incurable disease that struck first in the homosexual community. When it began to spread into the general population, gays became scapegoats for public fears. They were already stigmatized as "sinners." AIDS made them dangerous as well.

The responses ranged from demonstrations and protests against the gay lifestyle to violent attacks on individuals. For example, a gay college student in Wyoming was tied to a fence and beaten to death by three strangers he met in a bar. A gay couple in California died at the hands of two young gunmen they had never seen before.

So long as gays and other minorities are forced to live on the fringes of society, they will be vulnerable to violence. This is a fact of life for all minorities. Dr. Martin Luther King, Jr., once looked forward to a time when his children "would be judged, not by the color of their skin, but by the content of their characters." He knew that no law could make this happen. No presidential order or Supreme Court ruling could change people's prejudiced ideas.

However, Dr. King and others also knew that law could prevent discriminatory actions. Law could stop school districts from segregating children by race. It could prohibit racial or ethnic discrimination in the workplace. In other words, law could change the way people behave. In the cases of violence against gays cited above, the murderers were brought to court and convicted. The civil rights movement of the 1950s and 1960s began with that simple realization.

Leveling the Playing Field

The struggle to level the playing field for minorities began with the 1954 Supreme Court ruling against racial segregation in public schools. Civil rights activists then attacked the entire racial divide in the segregated South.

In states with racial segregation laws, the color line was drawn sharp and clear. Black people could not sit with whites in a movie theater or on a bus or train. They could not eat at the same restaurants, play in the same parks, or even use the same restrooms and water fountains.

Strict segregation reinforced the idea that black people were inferior to whites. This in turn led to more race hatred. The slow and painful process of racial integration was first met with violence and fear. People working for integration were arrested, beaten, and even killed. African-American homes, churches, and businesses were vandalized or burned.

With the law to help them, activists held marches, sit-ins, and boycotts. Slowly, the trappings of legal segregation gave way. Black people could sit in the front of the bus, or walk into a diner and order a hamburger. The "colored" and "white" labels on water fountains and restrooms disappeared.

As blacks and whites mingled more freely, some were able to look past the old stereotypes. Changed behavior slowly led to changed attitudes. Even in a reasonably well-integrated society, problems remained.

People of color were still overwhelmingly poor, limited to low-level jobs and ghetto neighborhoods. Schools in these neighborhoods were generally inferior and under-funded. They failed to prepare students for good jobs or college admission.

The Civil Rights Act of 1964 tackled these other forms of discrimination. It banned racial, religious, gender, and

The fight for African-American rights has been ongoing since slavery days. In the nineteenth century, Frederick Douglass amazed white racists with his quick intelligence, his dedication to the cause of abolition, and his ability to sway a crowd with stirring oratory.

national origin discrimination in the workplace and in public facilities. It established the Equal Employment Opportunity Commission (EEOC) to monitor hiring practices. The EEOC had the authority to set standards and to take legal action against employers who violated them. The very existence of EEOC was a direct challenge to white privilege. It put both employers and job-seekers on notice that a white face no longer guaranteed preference. Employers were required to make every effort to hire qualified minorities. Failure to do so could mean a hefty fine or other punishment.

The program worked. Companies that had hired only whites began recruiting in minority neighborhoods. Some set up their own equal opportunity offices to help minority applicants with the interview process. Some provided special on-the-job training programs. Despite white resentment and minority uncertainty, people of color began entering the work force in record numbers.

Minorities also began entering colleges and universities preparing for higher-paying, more prestigious positions. Special admission standards, or "minority preferences," opened admissions to students who might otherwise not qualify. This sometimes meant that qualified white applicants would be passed over for minorities with lower grade point averages and test scores. Unfair as this seemed, most people who were working for racial justice believed it was necessary.

In a 1965 speech at Howard University, President Lyndon B. Johnson explained why:

> You do not take a person who, for years, has been hobbled by chains and liberate him, bring him to the starting line of a race and then say, you are free to compete with all the others, and still justly believe that

you have been completely fair. We seek not just equality as a right and a theory, but equality as a fact and a result.[6]

Affirmative action fell short of creating equality as a fact and a result. It has often been criticized for what one attorney called "counting by race to achieve a society that no longer counts by race."[7]

In other words, it was not a perfect solution to the problem of racial discrimination. It was, however, a workable solution. It challenged white privilege while helping minorities become achievers rather than scapegoats and victims. Most important of all, it helped to bridge the racial divide. To many people, these achievements made affirmative action worthwhile in spite of its flaws.

4

The Power of Belonging

Everyone feels a need to belong. Group identity shapes an individual's sense of self-worth more than many people would like to admit. The need to be accepted by a group can lead to a number of destructive behaviors, including bigotry, scapegoating, and a willingness to put image over substance.

The Image of Beauty

In the early 1990s, a television commercial featured tennis player André Agassi extolling the virtues of a new camera. Agassi lobbed tennis balls while an imaginary camera clicked off one "snapshot" after another. As the action stopped, Agassi smiled out from the screen. "Image is everything," he said.

To many people, that statement applies to life as well as camera commercials. The American stereotype of beauty and success is a powerful image. People will make amazing sacrifices in the attempt to achieve it. For those who succeed the reward is popularity, admiration, and membership in the most exclusive group of all: the Beautiful People.

Everyone who has ever watched television or played with a Barbie doll knows "The Look": young, slim, blond, blue-eyed, athletic. Women and girls are slim and graceful. Men and boys are muscular and strong.

The Look is for sale everywhere, from the corner drugstore to the plastic surgeon's office. Hair coloring can turn dark hair to sun-washed blond. Diet plans can produce that vaguely bony look of top fashion models. Tinted contact lenses can make brown eyes blue. For those who really want to change their looks, plastic surgery can trim noses, tuck tummies, and generally make sure that nothing sags; that nothing is bigger or smaller than it ought to be.

For some people, the quest for The Look is not simply time-consuming and expensive; it is dangerous. Women trying to get pencil-thin have developed eating disorders such as anorexia nervosa and bulimia. Some have literally starved themselves to death. Men have done permanent damage to their bodies in an attempt to add muscle by using drugs called steroids. Steroids can also produce frightening personality changes, such as outbursts of anger and uncontrolled violence.

Perhaps the saddest part of all of this is that The Look is built from fantasies. With the exception of a few models, movie stars, and Barbie dolls, it does not really exist. It is a stereotype, an image. It is also a fashion; it changes with the times.

For example, seventeenth-century artist Peter Paul Rubens painted plump, well-rounded women. By today's

Young white women with "The Look" vie for the title of Miss Rheingold of 1956.

standards, they would be described as fat. In the 1950s, movie star Marilyn Monroe possessed the "perfect" female figure for her time.

Today's young women who diet to distraction trying to squeeze into a size six might be surprized to learn that Monroe wore a size twelve. Curves were the thing in the 1950s: full bust line, narrow waist, firm but rounded hips. These earlier images were no more real than The Look of today, but in their time they were equally powerful. They were also equally white.

Race and Body Image

For people of color, the sheer whiteness of The Look can be overwhelming. In a society that sees skin color first, the image is racist in a fundamental way. This is especially true for African Americans. The association of white with beauty and goodness and black with ugliness and evil is deeply embedded in the culture, as David Shipler pointed out:

> From the opening lines of Genesis, blackness has been woven into consciousness not as a mere color, but as a concept . . . darkness predates light and life. . . . Throughout the [Bible], the [contradiction between] light and darkness is linked to the contradictions of good and evil, truth and ignorance, glory and sin.
>
> The symbols [are present throughout] the books youngsters read and the films they see. In *The Wizard of Oz*, Glinda the Good Witch of the North is unabashedly dressed in white and the Wicked Witch of the West in black. In *Star Wars*, the ultimate villain, Darth Vader, is cloaked and hooded entirely in black.[1]

In the 1950s, psychologists studied the effects of black-white imagery on African-American schoolchildren. The psychologists wanted to show how racial segregation in schools damaged the self-esteem of black youngsters. They designed a simple but revealing study. A researcher would place black and white dolls in front of the subject and ask questions: Which is the good doll? Which is the bad doll? Which is the pretty doll, and which is the ugly one?

Again and again, the children associated white dolls with the good and beautiful and black dolls with the bad and ugly. A lifetime of being segregated and treated as inferior had taken its toll. This study became part of the proof in the Supreme Court case that outlawed school segregation.

In the late 1960s, African Americans began to create their own standards of physical attractiveness. "Black is beautiful" became the watchword. It was all right to have dark skin and kinky hair. Full lips and broad noses were neither ugly nor shameful.

Black neighborhoods came alive with colorful, African-inspired clothes and huge "Afro" hairdos. Black actors and celebrities reflected the new image on television and in movies. The effect was distinctive, compelling, and as "un-white" as it could possibly be. And it was beautiful.

"Black is beautiful" did not completely replace white standards of physical attractiveness, even among African Americans. However, it did mount a direct challenge to the connection between blackness and ugliness. In the process, it gave black people a new way to think about themselves, both as individuals and as members of a racial group.

The Power of "Us"

Group image is important to people of all races. Everyone wants to belong to the "right" groups. This is especially true among young people. The old saying about being known by the company one keeps is never more true than in the average American high school. Young people affirm their group identity in many ways: by where they sit in the lunchroom, who they invite to their parties, what clubs or sports teams they join, and the kind of clothes they choose to wear.

Status symbols are also important. Thanks largely to advertisers who realize this, teenagers in the twenty-first century live in a brand-name world. Athletes want to wear the most expensive shoes, drink the "right" sports drink, and wear team logos on their clothes. The computer crowd carries state-of-the-art laptops and owns all the latest software and video games. Each thing the members share affirms their common identity.

Status is not just important to individuals within the group. Each member also cares about the group's standing within the larger community. Belonging to a group that is envied and admired by outsiders is a badge of honor for all.

Unfortunately, one of the easiest ways to build the reputation of "us" is by finding a scapegoat group: "them." *We* are popular, pretty, athletic, or smart. *They* are a bunch of losers. Everybody wants to be like *us*. Nobody wants to be like *them*.

The scapegoat does not necessarily have to be an organized group. Loners and misfits are popular targets. So are racial and ethnic minorities. Both are easily identified, different enough to seem alien, and already marginalized by the larger society.

The Problem of "Them"

The scapegoating of out groups can easily turn brutal, or even deadly. The April 1999 shootings at Columbine High School in Colorado were the work of two boys who were part of a detested out group known as the Trenchcoat Mafia. In a report filed two days after the shootings, ABC newscaster Jonathan Dube tried to convey some sense of what happened that day:

They're different. They dress unusually, they act quirky, they keep to themselves.

But they're treated like scum—teased, insulted, [excluded]. And that ridicule finally got to two of them Tuesday, when Eric Harris and Dylan Klebold lashed out—firing automatic weapons across the school, tossing grenades, setting off pipe bombs, and killing 12 peers, a teacher and, finally, themselves.

"This is for all the people who made fun of us all these years," they said, laughing as they opened fire.[2]

After the tragedy, students at Columbine confronted the issue of cliques on campus. Cliques are part of life at most high schools, but at Colombine they were a special problem. There were dozens of them, and each little group created its own private world. As Jonathan Dube observed, at Columbine, "the cliques sound like the exaggerated stereotypes you'd find in a bad movie. Students say their lives revolve around the cliques."[3]

One senior gave Dube a frank explanation of the situation at Columbine:

"People are so worried about what their hair is going to look like, what they're going to wear, so worried that they look cool . . . It's a rat race inside the school to see who's going to be more popular. Everybody's thinking: Am I going to look cool for the popular kids? Are they going to accept me?"[4]

Living in the Cracks

The need for acceptance is strong among teenagers; the threat of rejection, a special kind of agony. In the search for acceptance, people of mixed racial ancestry and those involved in interracial relationships face special difficulties. Because they have crossed the racial divide, they may be rejected from both sides.

The standards have changed over the years. Some people who are accepted today would not have been accepted in an earlier time. In nineteenth-century America a marriage between white people of different ethnicities was cause for comment. For example, an Irish and Italian couple would be regarded as "mixed." In the 1950s, American soldiers stationed in Asia could cause a terrible scandal by bringing home Japanese or Korean brides. Black/white unions continue to be stigmatized, even in the twenty-first century.

The children of those unions, regardless of their appearance, were always classed as black in the past. In her book *Black, White, Other: Biracial Americans Talk about Race & Identity*, author Lise Funderburg explains:

> Slavery laws and social practices set a precedent—which survives to this day among many Whites and Blacks—of regarding anyone with a trace of African blood as black. Some states [formalized] it as the one-drop rule or *code noir* (black code) . . . . A paradox of the one-drop rule is that it is never a two-way street. The theory that any amount of "black blood" makes a person black [does not exist] within other racial groups, especially not Whites. One can be black and have "white blood" . . . but one cannot be white and have "black blood."[5]

In the 1990s, biracial people began claiming the right to define themselves. Some chose the race they most resembled, some the culture where they felt most comfortable, and some frankly described themselves as biracial or multiracial (people with more than two racial ancestries).

Golfer Tiger Woods made headlines by choosing an identity all his own. When he won the famous Masters

Golf great Tiger Woods has become a role model for others of mixed heritage because of his easygoing acceptance of his multiracial identity.

Tournament at the age of twenty-one, the media went into a frenzy. Every sports journalist and talk show host in the nation wanted to interview him. Aside from his spectacular talent, Woods was personable and charming. But some found his golden brown skin and faintly Asian eyes puzzling. People asked about his ancestry.

"Cablinasian," he told them. Woods made up the word when he was a child. It was the only way he could come up with to describe his racial heritage. Woods's father is black, American Indian, and Caucasian. His mother is half Thai and half Chinese. "Cablinasian" stands for CAucasian-BLack-INdian-ASIAN.

Tiger Woods's playful self-description sent a message: Being multiracial is not shameful, odd, or grim. It can be a source of pride, and even a source of joy. In a racially divided society, that is an important message to send.

5

Taking a Stand

According to U.S. government figures, the United States will be a truly multiracial society by the year 2050. This means that whites will no longer be the clear majority. Instead, they will become the largest minority in a nation of minorities.

Such a society can no longer afford to be racist. It would tear itself apart. Therefore, the quest for racial justice becomes more than a moral issue; it becomes a matter of survival.

A Place to Start

Getting beyond the racial divide will not be easy. It will take the combined effort of government, private organizations, and individual Americans. It will take honest efforts to recognize racism, understand it, and finally combat it.

It will also take courage. People who stand against racism can become targets of white supremacists and other racist groups. Some might face misunderstanding or ridicule from their friends and families.

It will take patience, especially from whites trying to build relationships with people of other races. Those who have suffered because of racial prejudice may not easily trust offers of white friendship.

Finally, it will take tolerance for one's own failings. Some people condemn themselves for even the smallest prejudiced thought. In a society where racism has been part of daily life for generations, such thoughts are understandable. Good intentions cannot wipe out a lifetime of exposure to racist ideas and images. It takes work to identify prejudices and deal with them, especially when those prejudices exist beneath the level of conscious awareness.

Identifying Unconscious Racism

Outspoken racism is easy to identify: Ku Klux Klansmen with their white-hooded robes, neo-Nazis with their swastika flags, the neighbor down the street who peppers his conversation with racist slurs. Unconscious racism is another matter. It is largely invisible. Even people who are consciously tolerant can harbor unrecognized prejudices.

In 1999, psychologists Anthony Greenwald and Mahzarin Banaji developed a test to detect unconscious racism. The Implicit Association Test (IAT) is somewhat like the black doll/white doll studies of the 1950s. However, modern computer technology has made it far more sophisticated and accurate.

Subjects are asked to associate good or bad words with

black or white images. They are instructed to work as quickly as possible, responding as the images and words appear on the monitor. The researchers found that the people tested associate good words with white images much faster than they group good words with black images. The reverse is also true; black/bad comes more easily than white/bad.

The results of IAT studies indicate that these associations have become part of the way people view their world. Test codeveloper Anthony Greenwald compares the situation to a garden: "You have the roots of weeds hiding under the soil and it's your job to make sure they don't grow and take over the flowers. That's a lot harder to do if you don't even know the roots are there."[1]

Rooting Out Prejudice

In the garden example, awareness of the roots does not eliminate them, nor does it pinpoint their exact location under the soil. To get to the roots, the gardener has to dig.

The same is true of prejudice. Simple awareness will not solve the problem. After awareness must come action, as the Anti-Defamation League (ADL) suggests in its guide to eliminating prejudice: "Whether the seeds [of prejudice] are planted around the dinner table, on the playing field, by the water cooler or in the boardroom, they can grow out of control. Even worse, when not uprooted, prejudices get passed on from one generation to the next and can fuel discrimination, victimization, bigotry and hate. With awareness, education and action, we can weed them out."[2]

Awareness of racial prejudice is not the same as awareness of racial differences. Even very young children are perfectly aware that human beings come in different colors. Prejudice begins with the meaning attached to those

Today's children are growing up in a multiracial and multicultural society. Learning to work and play with people from many different backgrounds is valuable training for the future.

differences: white is good, black is bad; all people not like "us" are inferior to us.

These associations are learned and can therefore be unlearned. This is the function of education: to help people identify, examine, and finally discard their own prejudices.

The next step is action—people working together to bridge the racial divide and create the kind of society Dr. Martin Luther King, Jr., envisioned. We should all work toward a society in which people would be judged for their character as individuals rather than their membership in any racial or ethnic group.

Chapter Notes

Chapter 1. What Is Racism?

1. "'Driving While Black' Is Not a Crime . . . So Why Are Incidents Like These Occurring Across the Country?" American Civil Liberties Union, n.p., n.d., <http://www.aclu.org/profiling/tales/index.html> (June 21, 2000).

2. American Anthropological Association, "Fact Sheet/OMB Directive 15," Office of Management and Budget, September 8, 1997, <http://www.aaanet.org/gvt/ombfact.htm> (June 23, 2000).

3. Bernard G. Campbell, ed., *Humankind Emerging* (Boston, Mass.: Little, Brown and Company, 1976), pp. 380–381.

4. "American Anthropological Association Statement on 'Race'," May 17, 1998, <http://www.aaanet.org/gvt/ombdraft.htm> (June 26, 2000).

5. Thomas Jefferson, *Writings* (New York: Library of America, 1984), p. 22.

6. Ibid., p. 266.

7. Ibid., p. 267.

8. Quoted in Eugenia Shanklin, *Anthropology & Race* (Belmont, Calif.: Wadsworth Publishing Company, 1994), p. 120.

9. Richard J. Herrnstein and Charles Murray, *The Bell Curve: Intelligence and Class Structure in American Life* (New York: Free Press, 1994).

10. Quoted in Elizabeth Hunter, "Seeing Our Racism: Relationships Remove the Lenses That Blind Us to White Privilege," *The Lutheran*, February 2000, p. 12.

Chapter 2. Stereotyping

1. Quoted in Paul R. Erlich and S. Shirley Feldman, *The Race Book: Skin Color, Prejudice, and Intelligence* (New York: Quadrangle, 1977), p. 10.

2. Quoted in Annie Murphy Paul, "Where Bias Begins: The Truth About Stereotypes," *Psychology Today*, vol. 31, May 15, 1998, pp. 52–55.

3. Jonathan Storm, "Ratings Race: A World of Difference in TV Viewing Habits of White, African Americans," *The Sacramento Bee*, April 19, 2000, p. F1.

4. Paul, pp. 52–55.

Chapter 3. Bridging the Racial Divide

1. Robert Jensen, "White People Need to Acknowledge Benefits of Unearned Privilege," Dawn/LAT_WP News Service, n.p., n.d., <http://www.purdue.edu/humanrel/rjensen.html> (October 10, 2000).

2. Quoted in Elizabeth Hunter, "Seeing Our Racism: Relationships Remove the Lenses That Blind Us to White Privilege," *The Lutheran*, February 2000, <http://www.thelutheran.org/0002/page12.html> (October 10, 2000).

3. David K. Shipler, *A Country of Strangers: Blacks and Whites in America* (New York: Alfred A. Knopf, 1997), p. 321.

4. Shirley Jackson, "The Lottery," *The Lottery and Other Stories* (New York: Quality Paperback Club, 1991), pp. 301–302.

5. The Public Eye, "The Scapegoat," Political Research Associates, 1997, n.p., n.d., <http://www.publiceye.org/tooclose/scapegoating-01.htm> (July 7, 2000).

6. Lyndon B. Johnson, "Address at Howard University's Commencement," *Public Papers of the Presidents: Lyndon Johnson*, vol. 2 (Washington D.C.: Government Printing Office, 1965), p. 636.

7. David Wagner, "Race-based Programs Are on the Defensive," vol. 13, *The World & I*, September 1, 1998, <http://205.178.185.71/index.shtml> (October 10, 2000).

Chapter 4. The Power of Belonging

1. David K. Shipler, *A Country of Strangers: Blacks and Whites in America* (New York: Alfred A. Knopf, 1997), pp. 232, 235.

2. Jonathan Dube, "Cliques Made Columbine a High School Hell," ABC News, April 23, 1999, n.p., n.d., <http://www.abcnews.go.com/sections/us/DailyNews/littletonboys990423.html> (January 18, 2000).

3. Ibid.

4. Ibid.

5. Lise Funderburg, *Black, White, Other: Biracial Americans Talk about Race & Identity* (New York: William Morrow, 1994), p. 13.

Chapter 5. Taking a Stand

1. Quoted in Claudine Chamberlain, "Roots of Racism Revealed," ABC News.com, 1999, n.p., n.d., <http://archive. abcnews.go.com...ourhead/allinyourhead_1 1.html> (June 15, 2000).

2. "Prejudice: 101 Ways You Can Beat It: A Citizen's Action Guide," Anti-Defamation League, 1999, p. 1, n.d., <http://www. adl.org/Prejudice/default.htm> (June 14, 2000).

Further Reading

Books

Chideya, Farai. *The Color of Our Future: Race in the 21ˢᵗ Century*. New York: Avon, 2000.

Ezekiel, Raphael S. *The Racist Mind: Portraits of American Neo-Nazis and Klansmen*. New York: Viking Penguin, 1995.

McCray, Carrie Allen. *Freedom's Child: The Life of a Confederate General's Black Daughter*. Chapel Hill, N.C.: Algonquin Books, 1998.

Tatum, Beverly. *Why Are All the Black Kids Sitting Together in the Cafeteria?: And Other Conversations About Race*. New York: Basic Books, 1997.

Internet Addresses

Anti-Defamation League of B'nai B'rith
<http://www.adl.org>

Center for Democratic Renewal
<http://www.publiceye.org/cdr/cdr.html>

Facing History and Ourselves: Survivors of the Holocaust
<http://www.tbssuperstation.com/survivors/FHO.html>

The President's Initiative on Race: Building One America in the 21st Century
<http://www.clinton2.nara.gov/Initiatives/OneAmerica/cevent.html>

Southern Poverty Law Center
<http://www.splcenter.org>

Index